和月伸宏

LOOKING BACK ON '96

(1) THREE CASES WHERE I REALLY LOST IT: ONE WHERE I JUST COULDN'T ACCEPT; ONE WHERE I JUST COULDN'T GIVE IN; ONE WHERE I JUST COULD NOT FORGIVE. (2) THREE CASES OF SINCERE REGRET...AFTER REALLY LOSING IT. IF I HADN'T LET ANGER TAKE CONTROL, IF I'D BEEN ABLE TO TALK ABOUT THINGS CALMLY, I MIGHT HAVE BEEN ABLE TO SOLVE THE PROBLEM WITHOUT HARMING RELATIONS OR TRUST. (3) ONE CASE OF ENLIGHTENMENT: WHETHER THEY'RE GOING POORLY OR WHETHER THEY'RE GOING WELL, THINGS ARE STILL ALL A RESULT OF ONE'S OWN ACTIONS.

Rurouni Kenshin, which has found fans not only in Japan but around the world, first made its appearance in 1992, as an original short story in ***Weekly Shonen Jump Special***. Later rewritten and published as a regular, continuing ***Jump*** series in 1994, ***Rurouni Kenshin*** ended serialization in 1999 but continued in popularity, as evidenced by the 2000 publication of ***Yahiko no Sakabatô*** ("Yahiko's Reversed-Edge Sword") in ***Weekly Shonen Jump***. His most current work, ***Busô Renkin*** ("Armored Alchemist"), began publication in June 2003, also in ***Jump***.

RUROUNI KENSHIN
VOL. 13: A BEAUTIFUL NIGHT
The SHONEN JUMP Graphic Novel Edition

STORY AND ART BY
NOBUHIRO WATSUKI

English Adaptation/Gerard Jones
Translation/Kenichiro Yagi
Touch-Up Art & Lettering/Steve Dutro
Cover Design/Sean Lee
Interior Design/Matt Hinrichs
Editor/Avery Gotoh

Supervising Editor/Kit Fox
Managing Editor/Elizabeth Kawasaki
Director of Production/Noboru Watanabe
Editorial Director/Alvin Lu
Executive Vice President & Editor in Chief/Hyoe Narita
Sr. Director of Acquisitions/Rika Inouye
Vice President of Sales & Marketing/Liza Coppola
Vice President of Strategic Development/Yumi Hoashi
Publisher/Seiji Horibuchi

Printed in the U.S.A.

Published by VIZ, LLC
P.O. Box 77010
San Francisco, CA 94107

SHONEN JUMP Graphic Novel Edition
10 9 8 7 6 5 4 3 2 1
First printing, March 2005

www.viz.com

PARENTAL ADVISORY
RUROUNI KENSHIN is rated T+ for Older Teen. It contains realistic violence and alcohol and tobacco usage. It is recommended for ages 16 and up.

www.shonenjump.com

SHONEN JUMP GRAPHIC NOVEL

Rurouni Kenshin™

MEIJI SWORDSMAN ROMANTIC STORY

Vol.13 A BEAUTIFUL NIGHT

STORY & ART BY
NOBUHIRO WATSUKI

CAST
緋村剣心（人斬り抜刀斎）
Himura Kenshin
(Hitokiri Battōsai)
神谷 薫
Kamiya Kaoru
相楽左之助
Sagara Sanosuke
明神弥彦
Myōjin Yahiko
巻町 操
Makimachi Misao
斎藤 一
Saitō Hajime
志々雄真実
Shishio Makoto
悠久山安慈
Yūkyūzan Anji

Once he was *hitokiri*, an assassin, called Battōsai. His name was legend among the pro-Imperialist or "patriot" warriors who launched the Meiji Era. Now, Himura Kenshin is *rurouni*, a wanderer, and carries a reversed-edge *sakabatō* to prohibit himself from killing.

THUS FAR

Kenshin has journeyed to Kyoto to block the machinations of Shishio Makoto, the man who took Kenshin's place as *hitokiri*. After him come Kaoru, Yahiko, Sanosuke... and a man who is out to kill Kenshin, Shinomori Aoshi. Along the way, Kenshin falls in with a girl named Misao and her mentor, Okina, former member of the Oniwabanshū and now-owner of an inn called Aoi-Ya. In a battle with Sōjirō—a member of Shishio's *Juppongatana* or "Ten Swords" corps of assassins—Kenshin's *sakabatō* is shattered, and so he acquires a new one, Shinuchi, from the son of the great swordsmith, Arai Shakkū. Next, Kenshin seeks out Hiten Mitsurugi-ryū master Hiko Seijūrō to obtain the ultimate secret of that school of swordsmanship... which Kenshin failed to learn when he deserted his studies 15 years ago. Meanwhile, Aoshi attempts to sell information on Kenshin to Okina and, when the latter refuses, Aoshi says he'll take his knowledge to Shishio. Okina fights to stop him, but Aoshi has rid himself of compassion and has become a veritable demon... and Okina falls. Misao declares herself *Okashira* or "head" of the Oniwabanshū, swearing to defeat Shishio no matter the cost.

Kenshin, armed with the secret called *Amakakeru Ryū no Hirameki*, meets with Sanosuke and Saitō and learns of Shishio's plans to set fire to Kyoto. Kenshin realizes that the plans must have been leaked on purpose, as a diversion from Shishio's real plot: to sail *Rengoku*, Shishio's ironclad warship, to Tokyo and to attack the capital from the seas. The three intercept Shishio at the port of Osaka, where Sanosuke sinks the warship with his explosives. The Oniwabanshū have saved the city of Kyoto from incineration, and the stage of battle moves on to Shishio's lair....

CONTENTS

RUROUNI KENSHIN
Meiji Swordsman Romantic Story
BOOK THIRTEEN: A BEAUTIFUL NIGHT

Act 103—After the Night

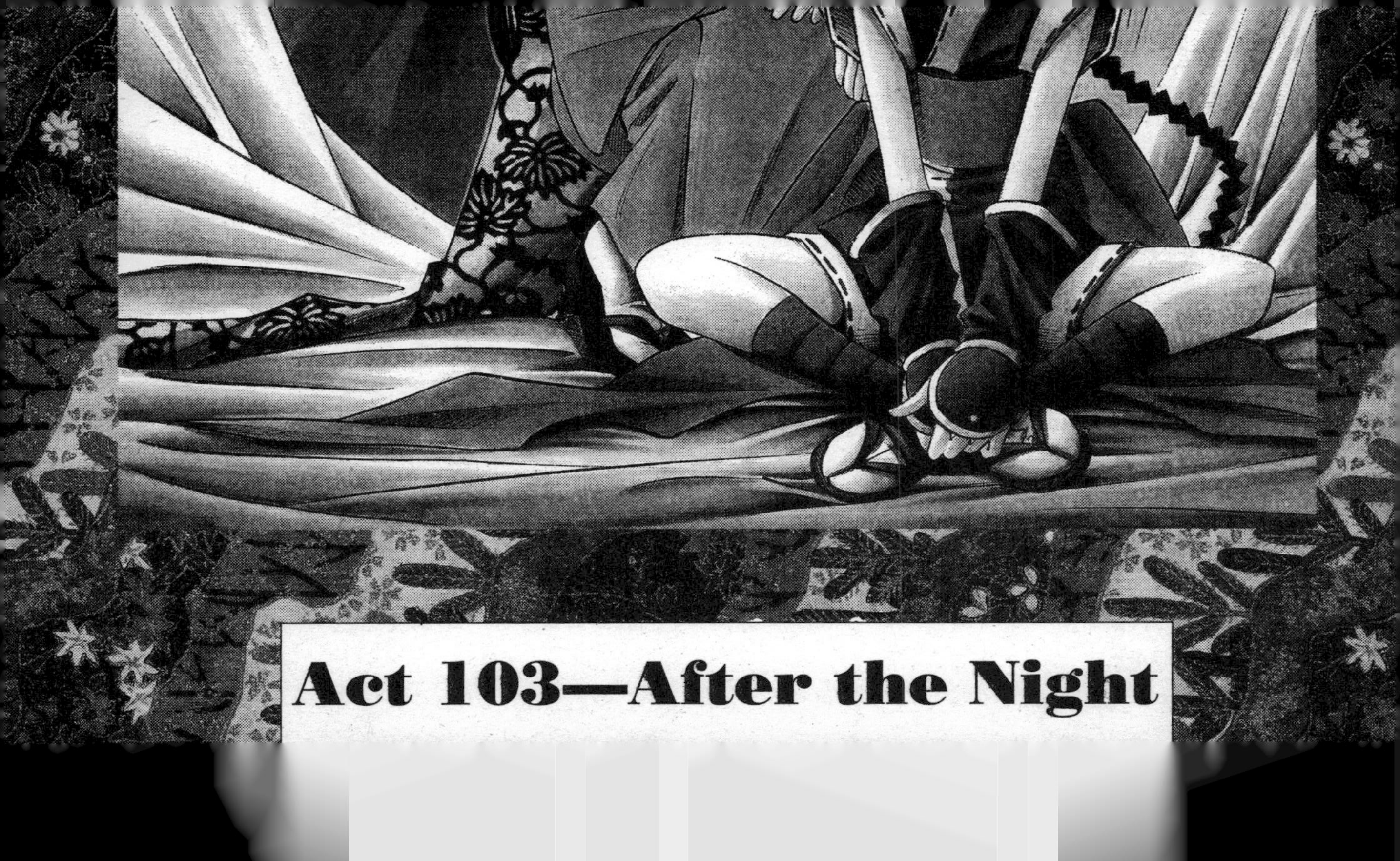
Act 103—After the Night

...BUT IT'S STILL 41 LIVES.
...HMPH.

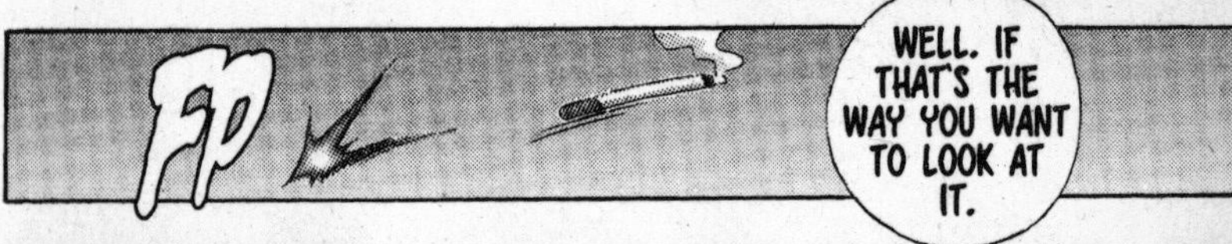
WELL. IF THAT'S THE WAY YOU WANT TO LOOK AT IT.
FP

I HAVE TO CLEAN UP THIS MESS BEFORE WE HIT SHISHIO'S LAIR. YOU TWO WAIT AT AOI-YA UNTIL YOU HEAR FROM ME.
HOLD ON!
EH?

MAYBE YOU TWO *ARE* FIGHTING TOGETHER FOR NOW...
...BUT GARBAGE IS STILL GARBAGE, EVEN IN KYOTO!

YOU WERE AT THE POLICE STATION SO LONG, SANO...
...OUGHTN'T YOU AND SAITŌ HAVE MADE *FRIENDS* BY NOW?

WAM
ME?! MAKE FRIENDS WITH THAT DOG?!
WHEN SHISHIO'S BEATEN, HE'S NEXT!

ANYWAY, I'M STARVING.
STOMP STOMP
HURRY AND GET US TO AOI-YA.
FINE, FINE.
EVEN IF YOU DID NEARLY KILL THIS ONE...

屋 葵
葵屋

LIFE TAKES SOME STRANGE TWISTS, DOESN'T IT?
AN ONIWABANSHŪ IN KYOTO... AND THEY'RE ON *OUR* SIDE!
葵屋
OH.
!
KENSHIN!
SANOSUKE!

HEH
HO! YAHIKO!
THEY MAKING YOU STAND OUTSIDE?
WHAT'D YOU DO NOW?
DROP DEAD!
I'M STAND-ING GUARD!
SSS
STEAM. NICE.

HEY KAORU!
KENSHIN'S BACK!

KLATTA
PEEEK
WHAT'S WITH THE SKULKIN' AROUND?
NOOOP!

SORRY TO HAVE WORRIED YOU...
...KAORU-DONO.
...MM.
YOU ACTUALLY GOT HER TO COME.
I MADE A PROMISE, DIDN'T I?

AND THE SECRET ...?
IS THIS ONE'S... MOSTLY.
NOW IT'S UP TO PURITY OF HEART.
AND HOW IS MISAO-DONO?
...YOU WON'T LIKE THIS...
THAT FOOL!
THE LETTER WAS OBVIOUSLY WRITTEN TO RAISE EVERY ONIWABANSHŪ IN KYOTO...
...BUT OF COURSE, WITH *HER* PERSONALITY, SHE'D HAVE TO TAKE IT ON *HERSELF*!
BLAST HER!
MISAO-DONO!

SHAME!
SHAME!
HOW COULD I LET AN ENEMY TAKE MY BACK?!
BAM
BAM
BAM
BAM
BAM
SHAME SHAME SHAME!
...
SHE'S BEEN LIKE THIS SINCE LAST NIGHT.

SHE WASN'T HURT...
...BUT IT WAS CLOSE.
N
SHE SEEMS TO BE TAKING IT HARD.
IT WAS A CRAZED WARRIOR IN CLOTHES COVERED WITH EYES, AND AN EYE MASK...
...WITH THE SYMBOL SHINGAN, "MIND'S EYE," ON IT. AND...I THINK HE WAS BLIND!
!

READ THIS WAY

USUI—THE "BLIND SWORD" OF THE JUPPONGATANA!
!
I'M TOLD HE'S ONE OF THEIR TWO BEST BY...
BROOM-HEAD
BUT... WAIT...IF HE TOOK YOUR BACK, WHY AREN'T YOU DEAD?!
MISAO!
MISAO-CHAN!
IT WAS STRANGE...

WOOM

ANJI. WHAT IS THE MEANING OF THIS?
ALL BUT KAMATARI AND HENYA'S UNITS ARE FLEEING.
ANY MORE FIGHTING IS MEANING-LESS.
I ASK WHY YOU INTERRUPT MY PLEASURES.
DEPENDING ON THE ANSWER, I MAY KILL EVEN *YOU*.
PWIK
USUI. YOU JOINED THE JUPPONGATANA ON ONE CONDITION...
...DID YOU NOT? WELL, SO DID I...*AND* ON THE SAME CONDITION.
"LIFE TAKEN, LIFE GIVEN."
THE RIGHT TO DO WHATEVER YOU WISH WITH THE ENEMY'S LIFE... NO MATTER WHAT YOUR ORDERS.
I DO NOT WISH...
...TO TAKE *ANY* LIFE ITHOUT EASON.

THEY STARED AT EACH OTHER WITHOUT MOVING FOR HALF AN HOUR.
AND SUDDENLY THEY LEFT WITHOUT SAYING A WORD.

THIS ANJI SEEMS A LITTLE DIFFERENT FROM THE REST OF SHISHIO'S MEN.
USUI DIDN'T WANT TO FIGHT HIM BECAUSE HE KNEW HE WOULDN'T GET AWAY UNWOUNDED.
HE'S THIRD-BEST OF THE TEN, THEY SAY.

WELL...AS LONG AS YOU'RE SAFE, MISAO-DONO.
...
YOU HAVEN'T HEARD A WORD, HAVE YOU.
...
!

SANO?
..."STRANGE TWISTS"...
...AND NOT JUST FOR YOU, KENSHIN.
IT'S TIME.
GRRIP
TIME TO TEST YOU WITH THIS FIST.

...
KENSHIN.
KENSHIN! HEY!!

OH... SORRY. WHAT IS IT?
I WASN'T DONE YET. THERE'S ANOTHER DANGEROUS GUY.

PWIK
MEANING YOU TOTALLY FORGOT.
RIGHT?
I DIDN'T TELL YOU BEFORE 'CAUSE I WAS AFRAID IT WOULD DISTURB YOUR TRAINING.

AOSHI?! IN KYOTO ?!
SHINOMORI AOSHI HAS GIVEN HIS VOW AS FORMER OKASHIRA TO KILL YOU...SO HE'S SIDED WITH SHISHIO MAKOTO...
葵屋
MORE THAN THAT!
...AND LEFT OKINA HALF-DEAD.

HE WAS MY MENTOR.
NOW HE IS MY ENEMY.

AND I...
GRIP
...WILL DESTROY HIM...

MISAO...
...DONO...

Rurouni Kenshin

Act 104—Tears

MISAO-CHAN!
BAM

KENSHIN-SAN?!
HF HF
GOOD TIMING!
ORO?
HURRY, EVERYBODY !!
HUH ?!
WH-WHAT ?!
...CAN SOME-ONE EXPLAIN THIS?
HELLO ?
THIS IS THE POLICE! IS THERE ANYONE HERE?!
!

WHAT- WHAT- WHAT- WHAT- ?!
...
OKINA!
WHAT'S HAPPENED ?!
UM... LADY ?

OKINA...
HE'S AWAKENED!!

...

Act 104
Tears
伸宏
和月

I'M AFRAID I'VE WORRIED YOU ALL.
I HOPE YOU'LL FORGIVE ME.
TUG
YOU LOOK LIKE A MUMMY!
HEY!
HIMURA-KUN.
I'VE A FAVOR TO ASK OF YOU.
—.....
OMASU.
YES?
I'M SORRY, BUT COULD YOU LEND ME YOUR SHOULDER?

HIMURA-KUN, HOW MUCH DO YOU KNOW...
...ABOUT WHAT AOSHI HAS BEEN DOING?
NOT MUCH.
BUT MISAO-DONO'S TOLD THIS ONE A LITTLE.
I SEE. THEN MY STORY WILL BE SHORT.
WHAT I ASK OF YOU CONCERNS AOSHI.

HE IS NO ORDINARY EVIL MAN.
I'VE WATCHED HIM SINCE HE WAS A CHILD.
HE HAS THROWN AWAY ALL SENSE OF GOOD AND EVIL. HE IS POSSESSED BY *SAIKYŌ*— "ULTIMATE POWER."
HE IS TOO MUCH FOR ME TO STOP.
LEFT ALONE, THE NUMBER OF HIS VICTIMS...
...WILL MOUNT ENDLESSLY BENEATH HIS BLADES.
HIMURA-KUN, I ASK OF YOU...
SHINOMORI AOSHI...
...MUST BE KILLED.

隠

READ THIS WAY

I UNDERSTAND THAT THIS WOULD BREAK YOUR VOW TO TAKE NO MORE LIVES.
BUT YOU ARE THE ONLY ONE WHO CAN DEFEAT AOSHI NOW.
ONLY YOU CAN DEFEAT THIS DEMON WHO HAS LOST THE HUMAN WAY.

THERE IS NO RESTING PLACE FOR A DEMON BUT DEATH.
THE ONLY WAY TO SAVE HIM, IS TO KILL HIM.
-BMP-

-BMP-
-BMP-
-BMP-
-BMP-
-BMP-
NEVER SHOW YOUR FACE BEFORE ME AGAIN.
-BMP-

READ THIS WAY

MY HEARTBEAT WON'T SLOW DOWN.
MY BODY WON'T MOVE.

I THOUGHT I'D ALREADY DECIDED.
I THOUGHT I'D BE
LIKE ICE.

HIMURA...
WILL YOU REALLY
KILL HIM?

WILL YOU TRULY...
...KILL AOSHI-SAMA,
HIMURA?

OKINA-DONO, YOUR WOUNDS...
...THEY LOOK AS THOUGH THEY'VE COME FROM HIS "SPIRAL-SWORD DANCE." IT'S A POWERFUL ATTACK. IF AOSHI WERE REALLY JUST A DEMON...
...YOU'D BE IN YOUR GRAVE NOW.

READ THIS WAY

AOSHI IS NO DEMON.
NOT JUST YET!

HE MUST HAVE HELD HIMSELF BACK AT THE LAST INSTANT.
MAYBE HE DIDN'T EVEN REALIZE IT. BUT IT SHOWS...

...THAT EVEN IF HIS *CONSCIOUS MIND* IS FOLLOWING IN THE WAY OF THE *DEMONS*...
...HIS *SOUL* IS STILL STRIVING TO BE *HUMAN*.

AOSHI'S RESTING PLACE IS NOT DEATH.
IT IS HERE.
AND THIS ONE PROMISES YOU...
...THAT HE WILL BE BROUGHT BACK.

HIMURA—
HIMURA-KUN...
MISAO-CHAN?

MISAO-DONO.
MISAO!
MISAO-CHAN...
MISAO-CHAN!
MISAO...?

WHAT...?

READ THIS WAY

OH.
I...
UM...
WHAT?
TP

IT'S GOOD TO HEAR...
...RIGHT, MISAO-CHAN?

YES.

...AND HERE WAS I, ABOUT TO BREAK HER HEART....
...
I ONLY HOPE I'M PROVED WRONG.
HIMURA-KUN.

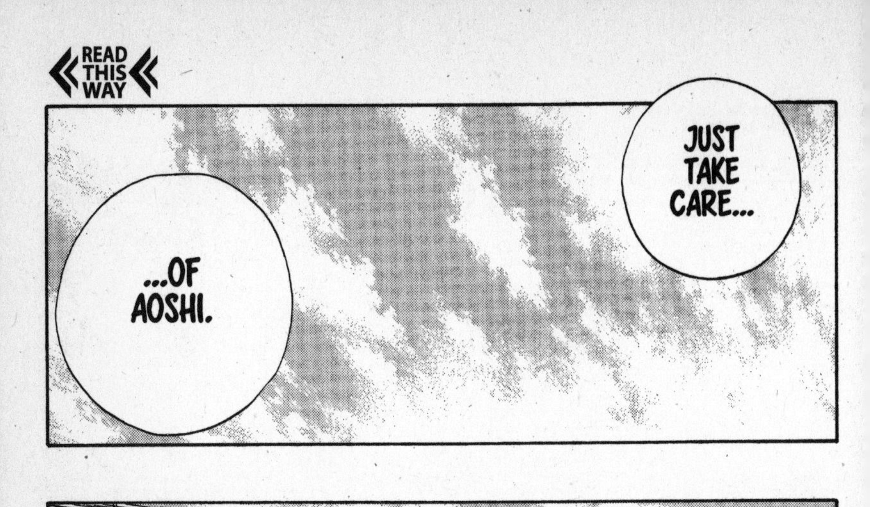
READ THIS WAY
JUST TAKE CARE...
...OF AOSHI.

葵屋
A MESSAGE?
YUH-HUH.
CAPTAIN FUJITA.
!

Rurouni Kenshin

Act 105—A Beautiful Night

...SO, THE ASSAULT ON SHISHIO WILL BE EARLY TOMORROW MORNING.
AN' TOO BAD, TOO, 'CAUSE I'M READY NOW.
I CAN'T BELIEVE THE BATTLE ADVANCED SO FAR WHILE I WAS ILL.
MM...
BUT NINE OF THE TEN JUPPONGATANA ARE STILL OUT THERE.
ONE MORE THING.
YOU HANG AROUND LIKE YOU BELONG HERE...
JAB
...BUT WHO ARE YOU?!

UH-HUH.
SCRATCH
SCRATCH
FEH. YEAH, ALL RIGHT.
I'M SAGARA SANOSUKE.
I'M A FRIEND OF KENSHIN'S.

MY QUESTION EXACTLY.
STARE
YOU DIDN'T *TELL* THEM ABOUT ME?
HEY!
WE'VE BEEN SO BUSY...
SORRY!

YOU DON'T BELIEVE ME?!
ARRH!
WHY SHOULD WE?
YOU LOOK SHADY.
YOUR EYES ARE SHIFTY.
MEN WITH HAIR STICKING UP ARE USUALLY TROUBLE.
LIKE CHŌ.

SANO...
...IS AMONG THE MEN THIS ONE TRUSTS MOST.
AHEM...

WELCOME, SON!!
PAT
...OH, SHUT UP.
WELL! OUR HIMURA-KUN HAS A LOT OF FRIENDS HERE!
LET'S DRINK TONIGHT, AS A SEND-OFF PARTY FOR TOMORROW'S BATTLE!!
OH NO, YOU DON'T!
YOU'RE STILL HURT! NO SAKE FOR YOU!!
POIT
POIT
TSK

YOUR OFFER IS APPRECIATED, OKINA-DONO, BUT WE'RE LEAVING EARLY TOMORROW MORNING.
AN EARLY DINNER AND SOME REST WOULD BE NICE.

...
隠

料亭
...

KENSHIN...
...KAORU-DONO?
YOU SAID YOU WANTED TO REST.
WILL YOU BE ALL RIGHT...?
ALREADY AN HOUR'S BEEN SPENT SLEEPING.
ONE HOUR? IS THAT ENOUGH?
YOU'RE UP LATE TOO, KAORU-DONO.
WHAT'S GOING ON?
OH, I JUST HAD TO GO—
DON'T ASK!
WAP
...

...SAY, KENSHIN?
MM?
WHAT YOU SAID THIS AFTERNOON...
YES?
AND THE SECRET...?
IS THIS ONE'S... MOSTLY.
NOW IT'S UP TO PURITY OF HEART.
THE "PURITY OF YOUR HEART."
AH.
BUT WHAT DOES THAT MEAN?
I'VE BEEN THINKING ABOUT IT, BUT...
IT'S FINE IF YOU DON'T UNDER-STAND.
IT'S NOT FINE!
NOT IF IT'S ABOUT YOUR LIFE AND DEATH!

AMAKAKERU RYŪ NO HIRAMEKI IS BATTŌJUTSU OF ULTIMATE SWIFTNESS...
...A TECHNIQUE FOR STRIKING WITH THE *SPEED OF A GOD.* ITS SECRET HAS BEEN LEARNED.

STILL, EVEN WITH SAKABATŌ, THE MASTER WAS NEARLY KILLED.
IT'S A TRULY DEADLY MOVE.

IF ONE'S SELF IS LOST, AS WAS IN THE BATTLES BETWEEN CHŌ AND SAITŌ...
...THIS TIME, IT'S CERTAIN, SOME-ONE WILL DIE.

AND YET, TO HOLD BACK IN FEAR OF *LOSING* THAT SPEED...
...RENDERS THE LEARNING OF THE SECRET MOVE ALL BUT USELESS.

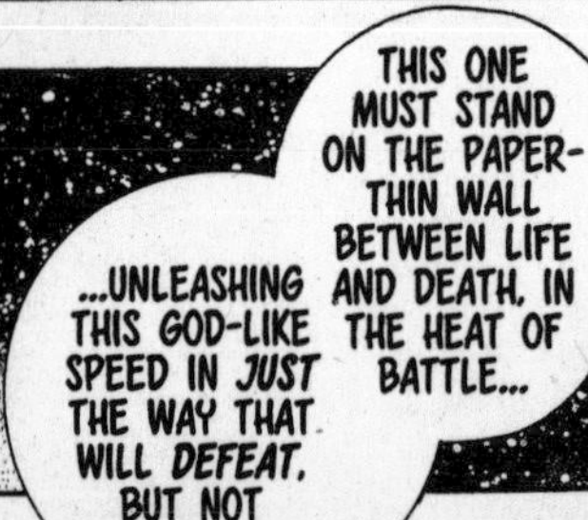

THIS ONE MUST STAND ON THE PAPER-THIN WALL BETWEEN LIFE AND DEATH, IN THE HEAT OF BATTLE...
...UNLEASHING THIS GOD-LIKE SPEED IN *JUST* THE WAY THAT WILL *DEFEAT,* BUT NOT *KILL.*

READ THIS WAY

AND IT'S NOT JUST MEGUMI AND I. WE ALL WISH FOR YOUR SAFETY.
SO...
SSP
HEY, KAORU !!
GOWN
BOOOWNNNG...!!
OW! WHAT ARE YOU DOING?!
SHUT UP AND COME OVER HERE!!
PSS
I'VE BEEN WATCHING YOU! HOW LAME CAN YOU GET?!
PSS
PSS
UMM...
...
PSS
WATCHING?! AND SINCE WHEN HAVE YOU BEEN A VOYEUR?!
PSS
PSS

WHAT'RE YOU WAITING FOR?! MEGUMI'S NOT EVEN HERE! K-K-*KISS* HIM, STUPID!
WHAT BUSINESS IS THAT OF YOURS?!
GET BACK INSIDE OR I'M TELLING TSUBAME-CHAN!
TSU-TSU-TSUBAME'S GOT NOTHING TO DO WITH THIS!
?
WOK
BOG
WOK
IT'S GOOD YOU SHOWED UP, YAHIKO.
THERE ARE THINGS YOU CAN SEE TO WHILE WE'RE GONE.
LIKE A RAY OF SUN...
GONE...?! YOU'RE NOT GONNA TAKE ME?!
OH!
TH
OF COURSE HE'S NOT!
IF YOU BOTH GET KILLED, WHO'LL PAY MY TAB AT AKABEKO?
IT'S GOTTEN WAY OUT OF HAND.

YOU WILL!!!
PAY OFF YOUR OWN DAMN TAB!!
JAB
PFF. NO WONDER YOUR DOJO'S SO SMALL-TIME.
YOU NEED TO WORK ON THAT ARGUMENT, SANO...

I'M COMING TOO, AND DON'T YOU SAY I'M NOT!
I HAVEN'T MISSED TRAINING ONE DAY SINCE I'VE BEEN HERE!
IF YOU DON'T THINK I'M STRONG, WELL, YOU'RE WRONG!!
IT'S OBVIOUS YOU'RE STRONG, YAHIKO.
WHY ELSE ARE YOU BEING ASKED TO STAY?

TOMORROW, WHEN WE'RE FIGHTING THE TEN SWORDS...
...SHISHIO'S MEN MAY SEE IT AS A CHANCE TO STRIKE AT AOI-YA.
WE'VE PREPARED A COUNTERMEASURE, BUT IF THAT HAPPENS, A BATTLE IS INEVITABLE.

AND THAT'S WHY WE NEED...
...TO KEEP SOME OF OUR BEST AT AOI-YA.

YOU'RE NEEDED HERE...
...TO DEFEND OUR FRIENDS!

YOU'VE-
-GOT IT!!
!!

DON'T YOU EVEN SWEAT IT!
AOI-YA IS SAFE WITH ME!
GRIP
BUT... UM...IN RETURN...
...ABOUT AOSHI-SAMA...
OHO!
WOW, YOU'RE SOMETHING ELSE.
WHAT HAPPENED TO THE TEARS?
...
BONG
WHAT TEARS?!?
NO TEARS! NO TEARS!
!
HIMURA-KUN.
AS MISAO SAYS, DON'T WORRY ABOUT US HERE.
JUST GO SCATTER SHISHIO AND HIS MEN!

HEH. SO EVERYONE'S AWAKE, AFTER ALL.
WE SHOULD'VE JUST HAD THE PARTY.
THE ARAI FAMILY, WHO GAVE THIS ONE...
Shake!
...THE SWORD, "SHIN-UCHI."
MASTER HIKO, WHO GAVE THIS ONE...
...THE SECRET, AMAKAKERU RYŪ NO HIRAMEKI.
THE TRUSTED FRIENDS...
...IN A FARAWAY CITY...
...AND THE TRUSTED FRIENDS GATHERED HERE.

YOU GIVE STRENGTH TO THIS ONE'S HEART.
THIS ONE HAS NOTHING TO FEAR.
WE'RE OFF.
...ARE YOU ALL PREPARED ?

KENSHIN.
I WANT US ALL...
...TO GO BACK TO TOKYO TOGETHER.
MM.

SHISHIO-SAMA. WE HAVE A REPORT FROM OUR INFORMANTS.
HIMURA, SAITŌ, AND SAGARA HAVE LEFT AOI-YA.
EXCELLENT. HŌJI, GATHER THE JUPPONGATANA HERE.

READ THIS WAY
IF I MIGHT FIRST SUGGEST A PLAN...
THERE IS NO *PLAN* FOR A *DUEL.*
UNLESS WE WERE TO PLAN THE ORDER OF COMBAT, OR...

—HŌJI.
WHAT ARE YOU THINKING?
THERE IS ONLY ONE THING I THINK ABOUT.
SHISHIO-SAMA'S ABSOLUTE VICTORY.

Rurouni Kenshin

Act 106
As an Abomination
SADOJIMA HŌJI
るろうに剣心
佐渡島方治
RUROUNI KENSHIN
伸宏
和月

"ABSOLUTE VICTORY"...
...YOU SAY?
INDEED.
ABSOLUTE.

IN THIS BATTLE WE SEND TEN—INCLUDING MASTER SHISHIO—AGAINST THREE.
IN NUMBERS AND STRENGTH, WE CLEARLY HAVE THE UPPER HAND.

OBVIOUSLY.
SO WHY ARE YOU UNHAPPY?

BECAUSE OUR ENEMIES ARE THE ELITE OF THE ELITE.
IF WE CLASH HEAD-ON, WE LOSE OUR LESSER WARRIORS, FROM CHŌ ON DOWN.
BUT IF WE ALSO BRING ONLY AN ELITE CORPS...
...HITTING THEM WITH THE THREE STRONGEST OF THE JUPPON-GATANA—AND ANJI...

...WE WILL HAVE SIX WARRIORS REMAINING ...
...TO COMPLETE THE ANNIHILATION OF WHOEVER REMAINS AT AOI-YA.
葵屋

!
IT'S GREAT!
PAP
QUESTION—WHY DID OUR GRAND PLAN FOR THE BURNING OF KYOTO FAIL?
EVER SINCE HIMURA BATTŌSAI ARRIVED IN KYOTO...
...THEY HAVE BEEN SUPPORTING HIM WITH THEIR NETWORK OF SPIES.
ANSWER—BECAUSE THE KYOTO ONIWABANSHŪ SCHEMED IN THE BACK-GROUND.
EVERYTHING WOULD HAVE GONE SMOOTHLY IF THEY DID NOT EXIST.
BEHIND OUR FAILURES WAS ONE, MUCH SIMPLER ONE—WE LET THEM LIVE.

NOW, BATTŌSAI IS NO FOOL.
NO DOUBT HE ANTICIPATES OUR ASSAULT ON AOI-YA IN HIS ABSENCE.
BUT HE IS STILL A SWORDSMAN.
IF HE'S CHALLENGED TO A DUEL, HE'LL NEVER EXPECT THE JUPPONGATANA THEMSELVES TO GO TO AOI-YA.
JUST AS YOU, WHO THINK SO MUCH LIKE OUR FOE...
...COULD ONLY CONCEIVE OF THIS AS A 10-TO-3 DUEL.
WE MUST NOT FORGET THAT OUR ULTIMATE OBJECTIVE IS TO CONQUER THIS NATION.
THAT IS SHISHIO-SAMA'S "ABSOLUTE VICTORY."
AND THAT REQUIRES RIDDING OURSELVES...
...OF HIMURA BATTŌSAI AND THE REST OF THEM...SIMUL-TANEOUSLY!

HŌJI.
WHEN DID YOU EARN THE RIGHT TO LECTURE ME?
I DON'T CARE IF YOUR STRATEGY IS BRILLIANT ...
...I TOLD BATTŌSAI THAT THIS WAS A DUEL.
SS
THE CODE OF THE SWORDSMAN ...
...WILL NOT ALLOW ME TO BEND THAT.

THE DUELS WILL NOT CHANGE!
NOW QUIT WASTING MY TIME AND GATHER THE JUPPON-GATANA!
...
SINCE I FIRST GAVE MY ALLEGIANCE TO THAT FIST...
...I HAVE KEPT TO ONE SECRET PROMISE.
HISTORY SHOWS THAT THE NATION WILL BELONG TO THOSE WHO ARE ABLE AND *WILLING* TO WIN...
...SO I PROMISED MYSELF TO DO WHATEVER I MUST TO ENSURE SHISHIO-SAMA'S ULTIMATE VICTORY.
ZOOP
TP
TP
I PROMISED I WOULD PLAY WHATEVER ROLE I MUST...

YES, EVEN IF IT BRANDED ME A COWARD AND AN UPSTART!
EVEN IF SHISHIO-SAMA HIMSELF CAME TO SEE ME AS AN ABOMINATION !!
GRIP
WITHOUT RENGOKU, THE JUPPON-GATANA ARE OUR STRONG CARD.
I CANNOT SERVE A LOSING PLAN THAT WILL NOT PLAY THAT CARD!
...
THIS IS THE FIRST TIME I'VE MET RESISTANCE...
...NOT ONLY FROM THE ENEMY, BUT ALSO FROM MY OWN DOG.
ENOUGH. SŌJIRŌ.
YES?

YOU GO AND GATHER THE TEN SWORDS.

SHISHIO-SAMA... THIS MEETING ...
...IS IT FOR THE NEXT BATTLE?
FIRST, THERE ARE THINGS THAT NEED TO BE SAID ABOUT THE LAST OPERATION.
FUNNY. I'VE BEEN WANTING TO ASK SOMETHING ABOUT THAT MYSELF.

I HEAR THAT THE BURNING OF KYOTO WAS JUST A DIVERSION.
WHICH WOULD MEAN THAT *WE* WERE JUST A SACRIFICE.
HEH
MMM... WHAT ABOUT THAT, SHISHIO-SAMA?
THAT WASN'T THE PLAN.
YOU WERE ALL SUPPOSED TO BE ON THE *RENGOKU*, STEAMING TO TOKYO.

BUT HŌJI HERE CHANGED THE PLANS WITHOUT ASKING, SAYING THAT THEY NEEDED TO BE MORE ELABORATE.
ISN'T THAT RIGHT...
...HŌJI?
...YES.
GLP
IT IS ALL...MY RESPONSI-BILITY.
BOW
PLEASE FORGIVE ME.

HA! I WONDERED WHY SHISHIO-SAMA WOULD ABANDON US!
THMM
...REALLY? SO THAT'S HOW IT WAS.
THEN HŌJI NEEDS TO BE PUNISHED.
VSH
GLP
WHY DON'T YOU TELL THE TRUTH, HŌJI?
LIES DON'T SNEAK PAST MY "SHINGAN" MIND'S EYE.
IF YOU TELL THE TRUTH, YOU WON'T GET HURT.
NNNN
I... HAVE NO IDEA...
...WHAT YOU MEAN.

GYAAAAH!
OOO... THAT MUST HURT.
URGH!
SHISHIO-SAMA...
PIF
NOW, DO YOU FEEL LIKE TALKING?
HHH
HHH

READ THIS WAY
I SPEAK... ONLY THE TRUTH.
THE JUPPON-GATANA WERE BETRAYED BY ME ALONE.
GG
AND I WILL PAY!
RRRIIIP
SEVEN NAILS FOR SEVEN BETRAYED... IF YOU WILL WASH AWAY...
...ALL SUSPICIONS OF SHISHIO-SAMA!
GUHH

NOW! YOUR ORDERS FOR THE NEXT BATTLE!
SO— USUI AND ANJI REMAIN HERE TO DUEL AGAINST BATTŌSAI !!
SAIZUCHI, FUJI, HENYA, KAMATARI, AND IWANBŌ WILL GO TO AOI-YA— AND BRING ME BACK THEIR *HEADS!!*

HŌJI. YOU WILL REMAIN HERE.
YOU WON'T BE ABLE TO FIGHT WITH THOSE FINGERS.
SHISHIO-SAMA...
TP
FROM NOW ON, I WILL LEAVE YOU ALL THE DIRTY WORK.
I'VE SEEN THE FIRE OF YOUR DETERMINATION.
IN RETURN, YOU WILL ALWAYS BE THE FIRST TO KNOW OUR VICTORIES.
RIGHT BY...
...MY SIDE.
HEH

THE FIRST DUEL GOES TO ANJI!

YOUR TARGET IS THE ONE WHO DESTROYED RENGOKU—SAGARA SANOSUKE!

HIS HEAD ALONE WON'T BE ENOUGH.
PULL OUT HIS SKULL... AND BRING IT TO ME!
SIX GATEWAYS.
THIS MUST BE IT.
THEN...
LET'S GO!!
WHAAAP

The Secret Life of Characters (33)

—Sadojima Hōji—

Most of the idea came from a certain "X-Men" character liked by Watsuki (it's where the name "Hōji" derives from). Not so much personality-wise, although he did give me a hint for the story. This character, from "X-Men," doesn't have any strong fighting powers, but he instinctively invents machines to help his allies. I thought it would be interesting to have a member of the Juppongatana who didn't fight directly, but who played more of a supporting role. Thus was Hōji born.

In the beginning, Hōji was just someone who gets surprised a lot. "This could get awfully dull," I thought, but then when I considered Hōji as Shishio's "Number Two," *then* the idea strummed the chords of my heart. (Just like Hijikata Toshizō and Shokatsuryō Kōmei!) Ideas started coming one after another, and soon Hōji became one of my favorite characters.

This may turn out to be a spoiler, but at the end of the Kyoto Arc, Hōji will be a pretty cool guy. I hope you're looking forward to it! (Watch the character not have any fans but me....)

People always think the model in terms of design is "Giant Robo," but that's just not true. This Hōji is 100% original to me! He's also one of the designs of which I'm most confident.

As touched upon in a previous volume, most readers seem to like "pretty" characters (male and female alike)–and probably with good reason!–but, for Watsuki, pretty's not enough. I think a mature manga artist should be able to draw villains and monster-types, too, and so I tend to put more effort into those kinds of characters. (Besides, if all the characters in a series are good-looking, the baseline for "good-looking" would get lost, and then how would we know who was supposed to be *really* beautiful and who was not?)

The only thing I *don't* like about the design for Hōji is the costume. I'd wanted to make it more like the European style authentic to those days, but when it came to finding the resources to do it, I couldn't seem to find any....

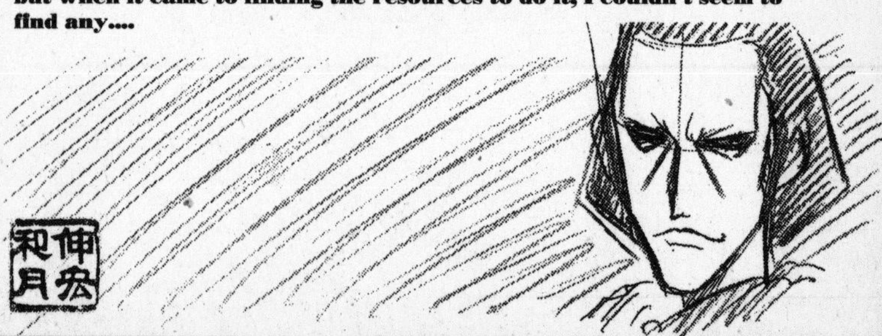

Act 107—The Bright King

MEETING HALL

I DON'T NEED YOU TO TELL ME THAT.
OF COURSE IT'S POSSIBLE.
HE MAY BE A FALLEN PRIEST, BUT HE DID LIVE THE WAY OF THE BUDDHA.
OF ALL THE TEN SWORDS, HE HAS THE MOST COMPASSION.
HOWEVER...

IN HIS CASE, WHATEVER COMPASSION HE MAY FEEL...
...IS FAR OUTWEIGHED BY HIS ANGER.
...
SSS
ANJI... THE "BRIGHT KING"...
...WILL TOLERATE NO ONE WHO IMPEDES HIS "SAVING" OF THE WORLD.

Act 107
The Bright King
るろうに剣心
RUROUNI KENSHIN
悠久山安慈
YŪKYŪZAN ANJI

INSTEAD OF POINTLESSLY WORRYING, YUMI...
...THERE IS A WAY YOU CAN MAKE YOURSELF USEFUL.
TP
TP
...
TP
TP
SOME-ONE...
...IS THERE.

WELCOME. I HAVE BEEN WAITING.
FROM HERE ON, THE BUILDING BECOMES A MAZE.
I WILL BE YOUR GUIDE. I AM KOMAGATA YUMI.
...USING WOMEN TO BRING DOWN OUR GUARD.
A COMMON TRICK. STAY ALERT.
!
TP
AND WHO'D FALL FOR A TRICK LIKE THAT EXCEPT YOU?
TP
...NO. SHISHIO ISN'T THAT CONNIVING.
!!
...
PLEASE. COME IN.

READ THIS WAY
IT'S NOT JUST A MAZE. IT'S A LABYRINTH.
ONE WRONG TURN MAY TRIGGER A STORM OF TRAPS.
EVEN FOR AN ASSASSIN'S FORTRESS...
...THIS IS AWFULLY ELABORATE.

...OH. I FORGOT ONE THING.
A MESSAGE FROM SHISHIO-SAMA.

THE DUELS ARE TO BE ONE-ON-ONE.
WE'LL PUT ONE MAN IN EACH ROOM. ONE OF YOU WILL CHOOSE AN OPPONENT EACH TIME.

THE OTHER TWO...
...CAN'T RAISE A HAND.

I LIKE IT.
MAN TO MAN! MY KINDA FIGHT!
GRIN
I'VE NO OBJECTIONS, EXCEPT THAT I HATE WASTING TIME.
CAN YOU GATHER ALL MY OPPONENTS AT ONCE?

AND YOU, HIMURA-SAN?
FINE. BUT THIS ONE WON'T JUST SIT AND WATCH...
...IF SOMEONE TRIES TO FINISH OFF THE LOSER.
SO, A DUEL, YES.
KILLINGS, NO.
REALLY.
HEH
SUCH A SOFT MAN.
HERE'S YOUR FIRST FOE...
...IF YOU PLEASE.

!
FUDŌ MYŌ-Ō, AKA ACALA...
IMPRESSIVE. IS THERE A PRIEST AMONG THE JUPPON-GATANA?
YEAH.

ONE WHO STRAYED FROM THE PATH.
A FALLEN PRIEST.
THERE ARE THINGS I WANT TO ASK HIM.
I'LL BE FIRST UP.
TP

KOMAGATA-DONO, WHO IS THIS...?
MYŌ-Ō OR "BRIGHT KING" ANJI.
HE IS VERY GOOD.
ANJI. THIRD-STRONGEST OF THE JUPPONGATANA, AND THE ONE WHO SAVED MISAO-DONO.
AND—
GRIP

READ THIS WAY
WHATEVER HE IS, BE CAREFUL, SANO.
THERE'S SOMETHING ABOUT HIS PRESENCE ...
I'VE WANTED TO SEE YOU AGAIN, BUT I DIDN'T THINK IT WOULD BE LIKE THIS.
HO.
IT'S BEEN A MONTH.
...NOR DID I.
THE WORDS YOU SPOKE IN SHIMOSUWA OF YOUR HATRED FOR THE MEIJI GOVERNMENT WERE ALL FALSE.
YOU DISAPPOINT ME.
WELL, YOU DISAPPOINT ME!
YOU FRAUD OF A PRIEST!!

HOW CAN A PRIEST AID SHISHIO IN HIS BLOODSHED?!
WHAT HAPPENED TO YOUR "MISSION OF SALVATION"?!

NOTHING HAS HAPPENED.
THE FIRST STEP IN THE MISSION...IS DESTRUCTION.

WHAT?!
FOOL.

DO YOU BELIEVE SAVING THE WORLD MEANS RESCUING PEOPLE FROM SUFFERING?

NOT THAT I BLAME YOU. WHEN I WAS BLINDED BY BUDDHISM, I THOUGHT THE SAME.

BUT NOW I SEE THE TRUTH.
THIS WORLD CONTAINS TOO MANY BEASTS AND SCAVENGERS, THOSE WHO ARE NOT WORTH SAVING...

...AND THOSE LOWLY BEINGS WITH HUMAN FACES AND BEASTLY SOULS...
...ROB THE PURE-SOULED OF THEIR RIGHTFUL FUTURES.
GNG
FROM THE CHAOS OF BAKUMATSU COMES THE POWER OF MEIJI.
BUT, IN THE CHANGE, SOULS HAVE TURNED ROTTEN. THERE ARE FAR TOO MANY BEINGS UNWORTHY OF LIFE.
TO SAVE THOSE WHO NEED TO BE SAVED...
...THE UNWORTHY MUST BE CLEARED AWAY.
FOR THIS DUTY, I HAVE JOINED THE JUPPONGATANA.
I HAVE BECOME THE INCARNATION OF FUDŌ MYŌ-Ō!

I WILL WASH THIS WORLD CLEAN IN BLOOD AND FIRE!
I WILL PUNISH THE CORRUPT AND LEAVE A WORLD OF PURE SOULS!
THIS IS THE TRUE MISSION!
CAN YOU UNDER-STAND, SAGARA SANO-SUKE?
NOT ONE WORD, FOOL!
GUESS MAYBE I DIDN'T STUDY ENOUGH BUDDHISM!
BUT I KNOW ONE THING.
I CAN'T...
GRIP
...SAY THAT I LIKE...
...YOUR DAMN MISSION MUCH!!

SANO!!
OORAH!!
WE SAW IT THAT TIME WITH RENGOKU...
!
THIS IS THE THIRD TIME. IT CAN'T BE BY CHANCE.

ON THE WAY FROM SHIMOSUWA TO KYOTO, I TRAINED ON 100 STONES.
I'VE MASTERED THE ART OF THE "TWO LAYERS."
KRUMBLE
KRUMBLE
SURRENDER, ANJI.
I DON'T WANT TO *KILL* YOU WITH WHAT I *LEARNED* FROM YOU.
KILL ME...?
YOU BOAST, LAD.

!
ALL I TAUGHT YOU WERE THE BASICS.
THIS IS MASTERY.

Rurouni Kenshin

Act 108—The Difference in Strength

Act 108
The Difference in Strength

...
THE "MASTERY OF TWO LAYERS" WITH BOTH ARMS AND LEGS...
...AND HIS LEFT ELBOW INSTEAD OF HIS FIST?
SANO!

!
NKH!

SHUT UP!!
DO YOU WANT TO SWITCH?
FFFFFF

I DON'T BLAME YOU FOR BEING BLIND TO MY MISSION.
JUST KNOW...
...THAT IT IS THE BLIND WHO MUST DIE.
TPP
NO MISTAKE— HE CAN USE BOTH ARMS... HIS LEGS...
...AND PROBABLY EVEN HIS HEAD IN THE USE OF THE "TWO LAYERS"!
I'VE GOT ONLY MY RIGHT FIST...
...AND ONLY ONE MOVE...

BUT I CAN'T RUN AWAY!!

...I THOUGHT YOU WERE AN INTELLIGENT MAN.
FFFF
YOU'VE OVER-ESTIMATED HIM.
I SAID, SHUT UP!
ARR!

SANO!!
DON'T BE INTIMI-DATED!
EVEN IN KENJUTSU, TWO SWORDS DON'T ALWAYS BEAT ONE!
YOU DON'T HAVE TO BE INTELLIGENT TO DEFEAT HIM!!
I TELL YOU, WITH "FRIENDS" LIKE THESE...
!

BUT...
...I DO SEE A WAY!
GRIP
HIMURA-SAN.
THE DUEL IS ONE-ON-ONE. NO AIDING HANDS.
YES. THAT'S WHY IT WAS MOUTH ONLY.
STILL THE SLICK TALKER, AREN'T YOU.
DIS-AGREEABLE MAN.
♫
TP
A WAY TO WIN? POOR FOOL.

FOR YOU, THERE IS NO SUCH THING.
MAYBE NOT...
...THEN AGAIN, MAYBE SO!!

VYOO
VNN VNN
HERE!
!

JUST AS I THOUGHT! YOU MASTERED THE TWO LAYERS AND TURNED YOUR BODY INTO A MASS OF *MUSCLES*...
BUT NOW THOSE MUSCLES ARE WEIGHING YOU DOWN, NOT LETTING YOUR *BODY* FOLLOW YOUR *FIST!*
THE TWO LAYERS CAN TAKE DOWN ANYONE WITH ONE BLOW!
DOESN'T MATTER IF IT'S JUST MY RIGHT FIST— THE FIRST ONE TO LAND A BLOW, *WINS!!*
ORAAH!!
IT'S IN!

HE STRUCK FROM THE OPPOSITE SIDE OF YOUR ATTACK...

...DISRUPTING THE FORMATION OF THE LAYERS...AND HAMMERING YOUR OWN FORCE *BACK* AT YOU!

THIS IS WHAT YOU CALL...
...MASTERY.
I WILL SAY IT...
...ONE MORE TIME.
NGH!
SANO!

RIP
DOM
SO CLOSE...
SIGH
I WASN'T SURE THERE WAS A WAY TO BLOCK THOSE BLOWS...
B BMP
!!

SO MUCH FORCE... WITH JUST A SKIM...
HUH
HUH

...THE SAME TECHNIQUE I LEARNED...
...BUT SO DIFFERENT FROM MINE...

TURN BACK.
THIS TIME, I WILL LET YOU GO.

...
HUH
HUH

TAKE YOUR FRIEND'S OFFER AND SWITCH WITH HIM.
YOUR ALTERNATIVE IS DEATH.

HEY. PRIEST.
SHISHIO-SAMA SAID TO KILL HIM.
THE DECISION IS MINE!
I HOLD THE RIGHT OF SEISATSU YODATSU!

"SEISATSU YODATSU"... YOU MEAN...
...THE POWER TO CHOOSE WHO LIVES AND DIES?

PFF. SO MUCH TALK ABOUT BEING "MYŌ-Ō" HAS YOU STARTING TO THINK YOU'RE ACTUALLY A GOD.
CONCEITED PUNK.
...

WAS IT SHISHIO WHO GAVE YOU THIS "LIFE OR DEATH" POWER?
IF SO, HE MUST BE THE GREATEST GOD OF ALL!
HE GAVE ME NOTHING. I'M AIDING HIM BECAUSE WE BOTH SEEK THE DEATH OF THE MEIJI GOVERNMENT.
BUT IF THE NEW WORLD SHISHIO CREATES DOES NOT SUIT MY MISSION...
...THEN I WILL BECOME HIS ENEMY, AND DESTROY THAT WORLD AS WELL.

!
AND YOU'LL JUST KEEP DESTROYING FOREVER?

I HATE THE MEIJI GOVERNMENT, TOO, AND I DON'T THINK I'LL GET OVER IT.
SOMETIMES I FEEL LIKE JUST KNOCKING IT ALL DOWN.
惡

BUT THERE ARE PEOPLE STRIVING TO LIVE DECENTLY IN THIS WORLD...
GNG
...AND OTHERS WHO *BELIEVE* IN THOSE PEOPLE AND *FIGHT* FOR THEIR FUTURE!

IT'S YOUR OWN BUSINESS IF YOU WANT TO GIVE UP ON THE WORLD, ANJI.
BUT AS LONG AS THERE ARE PEOPLE WITH HOPE, I WON'T LET YOU PLAY GOD!
I WON'T LOSE THIS FIGHT.
I CAN'T LOSE THIS FIGHT!!

READ THIS WAY

CAN'T WE STOP THIS?
IT WON'T BE JUST A KILLING MATCH NOW...
IT'LL BE A BLUDGEONING.

"I CAN'T LOSE..."
HE SAID THE SAME THING WHEN WE FOUGHT.
BUT THIS TIME THAT "CAN'T"...
...CARRIES MORE WEIGHT.

Rurouni
Kenshin

Act 109

Conviction of the Fist

伸宏
和月

HOHHH!!
RAHHH!
DSH

GNNN NN MMNN
...
WUMPH

YOHH!
TON TON TON TON TON TON TON
SINCE SKILL DOESN'T WORK, I GUESS HE'S GOING FOR QUANTITY.
BUT AGAINST THAT WALL OF MUSCLES, I DON'T SEE ANY HOPE.
IT'S ALL IN THE MASTERY OF THE TWO LAYERS.
LOOK AT ANJI. CONCENTRATING ON JUST HIS RIGHT HAND.
SANO KNOWS THAT.
THAT'S WHY HE'S NOT USING THAT HAND AT ALL.

I KNEW IT!
YOU DON'T HAVE THE GUTS TO FINISH THIS PRETENDER!
YOU'RE STILL SOFT AS ANY PRIEST! FORGET THAT HE LEARNED FROM YOU!
QUIT WASTING OUR TIME!
THM
HH
HH
HH
HAVE YOU HAD ENOUGH...
...OF THIS FUTILE EFFORT?
YOU LEARNED THE BASICS OF THE MASTERY OF TWO LAYERS IN JUST ONE WEEK, WHERE IT TOOK ME A FULL MONTH.
IT'S A SHAME TO HAVE TO KILL A MAN LIKE YOU. YET I MUST.

YOU WILL FEEL THE RIGHTEOUSNESS OF MY MISSION WITH YOUR BODY...
...AND DIE.
IT'S ABOUT TO END.
IF YOU WANT TO STOP THEM, DO IT NOW.
YOU WORRY A *LOT* ABOUT SANO, DON'T YOU.
...DON'T BE STUPID.
SIZZLE
I'M JUST WORRIED ABOUT WHAT HIS DEATH WILL DO TO YOUR MORALE.

READ THIS WAY
THEN DON'T.
SANO'S NOT GOING TO DIE.
DO IT, THEN!!!

AT LAST!
NOTHING STOPS ANJI WHEN HE SWINGS THAT FIST!!
WATCH MY MISSION FROM THE CHASMS OF THE AFTERLIFE!

READ THIS WAY
—....
IT'S DONE.
NAMU AMIDA BUTSU...
SHH

!
SORRY. IT'S TOO EARLY TO PRAY FOR ME.
YOU CAN'T...
...HAVE NEUTRALIZED IT?!
HYOHHHH!

AND NOW ...
...IT IS DONE!!!

WELL.
YOU WON, ALL RIGHT.
BUT IT WAS A PLAIN, STAB-IN-THE-DARK MIRACLE.
...HALF TRUE.
HF
HF
TRYING TO COUNTER ANJI'S RIGHT WITH MY OWN MASTERY OF TWO LAYERS WAS A GAMBLE.

BUT I DIDN'T JUST LUCK INTO IT AT THE END.
WHAT I HAD IN THIS FIST WAS CONVICTION.
IT'S WHY I RISKED MY LIFE TO MASTER THE TWO LAYERS TO START WITH.
STAB IN THE DARK, YES.
MIRACLE, NO.
...ANJI...
...HE CAN'T BE...
TP
DON'T WORRY. HE'S NOT DEAD.
I HOPE.
BUT HE DID TAKE A DIRECT HIT FROM THE "TWO LAYERS," SO HE PROBABLY WON'T BE WAKING UP FOR A WHILE.

HF
HF
HF
!!!
HF
HF
N... NO...
THE BLOW, IT...LANDED PERFECTLY...

READ THIS WAY
HUK
HUH
GNG
HUH
...
A MEMORIAL TABLET ...?

B-BMP
B-BMP

READ THIS WAY

IT'S OVER, ANJI.
THE MATCH IS OVER.
!

HH
HH
TO BE HONEST, BASED ON PURE STRENGTH...
...YOU'RE A FEW LEVELS BEYOND SANO.
BUT, IN SANO'S FISTS, THERE'S NOT ONLY POWER...
...BUT THE DESIRE TO *KEEP FIGHTING* FOR THOSE HE PROTECTS.

THAT DESIRE BROUGHT HIM POWER...
...BEYOND YOUR MISSION TO "SAVE THE WORLD."

ANJI.
YOU SAVED MISAO-DONO'S LIFE.

THIS ONE CANNOT BELIEVE YOU LIVE ONLY FOR DESTRUCTION.

WHY DID YOU DECIDE TO BECOME THE "FUDŌ MYŌ-Ō" ACALA BUDDHA?

AND WHO DOES THIS TABLET BELONG TO...
...THAT YOU HOLD IT TO YOUR CHEST, EVEN IN BATTLE?

IT ALL STARTED TEN YEARS AGO...

...ON THE NIGHT THEY DESTROYED THE TEMPLE...

"FREE TALK"

Long time no see. Watsuki here. There's a rumor on the streets that after the conclusion of the Kyoto stories, "RuroKen" is going to end. Not true! So long as there's reader support, Watsuki will keep going. And now for the usual nonsense....

"Samurai Spirits 4: Amakusa Kōrin ('Amakusa's Descent')." At the time of this writing I've only played it four times, but it's VERY GOOD!!! They take into account beginners and bad players, lowering the difficulty of the computer and allowing for 120% enjoyment. The system's become even more complex—which startled me a little—but that's fun, too. I'll be hooked on "SamuSupi" for a while (with "Rasetsu" Genjūrō, this time 'round). Speaking of fighting games, the polygon "Kenshin" is out. I haven't played this one yet, but it looks pretty good. There seem to be some hidden elements, so those of you who have the extra money to spend, give it a try.

Sunsets have really been getting to me lately...especially the sunsets of this season (winter), and specifically the ones that come at the end of the year. On this certain TV station in Tokyo, during the late-night programming after scheduled broadcasting, various shots of sunsets are shown as captured by weather-report cameras. I could look at them forever. Really, I'd like to watch them live, all night long, but unfortunately, I don't have the time. For now, my plan is to stay in a really high hotel room (elevation-high, not price-high) and just look at them—in Shinjuku or Ginza or maybe from a currently trendy seaside resort.

My reasons for liking sunsets isn't just because they're beautiful, but, because for me, they embody the end of a day, the end of a year, the way people struggle to keep going, even when they feel they've reached the end. (Know what I mean?) Take some time to watch a sunset—really watch it. You'll "get it" too, in your own way.

Okay, see you next volume!

Haibutsu Kishaku

In the fourth year of Keio—the first year of Meiji—the new government, in order to create a state religion and reduce the power of Buddhist priests, ordered the separation of Shintō and Buddhism. The population, though, interpreted this as an order to abolish Buddhism, and a storm of hostility was sparked that led to the destruction of many temples, relics, and texts. This is what's meant by "Haibutsu Kishaku"...a storm that now rages fiercely in one man's body.

Act 110—A World Not Worth Saving

Act 110
A World Not Worth Saving

IN THE SECOND YEAR OF MEIJI, IN THE SNOWY REGIONS OF EZO (HOKKAIDO), THE BATTLE BETWEEN THE ARMIES OF THE GOVERNMENT AND THE SHŌGUNATE GOES ON.
THIS MOUNTAIN-VALLEY VILLAGE HAS ALREADY BEEN SECURED BY MEIJI, THOUGH, AND IS WELCOMING SPRING.
JŪGAKU TEMPLE
十楽寺
WHEE!
WHEE!
ZG
ZG
NYEH
BWAH
UM, TASUKE, GORŌ ISN'T...
SS

HEY TASUKE!! QUIT PICKING ON GORŌ!!
AND GORŌ, STOP CRYING ABOUT EVERY LITTLE THING!
PAP
NOW HURRY UP AND PLANT SEEDS! PLANT!
WAAAH!
YOU TOO, PRIEST! WHEN YOU SCOLD, YOU HAVE TO MAKE YOURSELF AN OGRE AND SCOLD WELL!
YOUR FACE IS TOO *KIND*, FOR STARTERS!
RATTLE
MM.
I'M NOT SO GOOD AT BEING MEAN.
I'M SORRY.

WELL.
THAT'S WHAT MAKES YOU WHO YOU ARE.

SISTER TSUBAKI!
WHAT, WHAT?! WHAT NOW?!
WAAH!

A SNAKE!
WHY DIDN'T YOU SAY SO?!
DASH

...

PRIEST ANJI?

IS PRIEST ANJI HERE?

!

THE VILLAGE CHIEF...

...LEAVE THE VILLAGE?
AS I SAID.

YOU KNOW OF THE HAIBUTSU KISHAKU.
WE DECIDED AT THE MEETING TO FOLLOW THE GOVERNMENT'S POLICY... AND RAZE THIS TEMPLE.
BUT... PLEASE...I DON'T CARE ABOUT MYSELF, BUT WHAT WILL THE CHILDREN DO?
THESE CHILDREN LOST THEIR PARENTS IN THE BOSHIN WAR, AND HAVE NOWHERE TO...

OF COURSE THEY CAN LEAVE WITH YOU.
OR RATHER... THEY WILL *HAVE* TO LEAVE.
MY PREDECESSOR AS CHIEF, TSUBAKI'S FATHER, SIDED WITH THE SHŌGUN DURING THE BOSHIN WAR.
CONSEQUENTLY, THE NEW GOVERNMENT FEELS *LITTLE FONDNESS* FOR US.

FORTUNATELY, I HAVE A FRIEND WHO KNOWS AN OFFICIAL.
IF I PLAY MY CARDS RIGHT, THE SITUATION MAY BE CHANGED.
TO BE BLUNT, THAT MEANS THAT THIS TEMPLE, THIS PRIEST...
...AND THOSE ORPHANS ARE IN THE WAY!
ANJI...
PRIEST!
PRIEST!
THEY WON'T REALLY PULL DOWN THE TEMPLE?
WHERE WILL WE LIVE?
I'M SORRY, ANJI...
BECAUSE OF MY FATHER...

!
YOU HAVE NOTHING TO APOLOGIZE FOR.
I KNOW THAT YOUR FATHER DID WHAT HE THOUGHT BEST TO BRING PEACE QUICKLY.
TP
DON'T WORRY, ANY OF YOU. JUST ENJOY BEING ALIVE.
SUCH WAS THE WISH OF YOUR FATHERS AND MOTHERS.
IT'S MY WISH, TOO.
BUT IF WE STAY HERE, WE WILL BE A BURDEN ON THE VILLAGE.
WE MUST MOVE ON TO A NEW LAND... BUT WHERE?
I SAY TOKYO! TOKYO IS GREAT!
YAAY!!
I SAY HAKODATE!
HAKODATE'S IN THE MIDDLE OF THE WAR, STUPID!
?
NO! KYOTO!

BUDDHA, THESE CHILDREN HAVE SUFFERED TOO MUCH.
PLEASE GRANT THEM A HAPPIER FUTURE.
PLEASE GIVE THEM...
CHIEF... DO WE HAVE TO BE SO EASY?
MM?
IT'S JUST A POOR PRIEST WITH NO PROPERTY IN A WORN-DOWN TEMPLE, WITH FILTHY KIDS WHO'VE NO PARENTS.
NOBODY'S GOING TO *COMPLAIN* ABOUT HOW THEY'RE TREATED.
...YOUR PRO-TECTION.
THE MEIJI GOVERN-MENT'S FUNDS HAVE A LIMIT.
HEH
IF YOU WAIT TOO LONG, THE OTHER VILLAGES WILL GET ALL THE PRIVILEGES.
HM...

TRUE ENOUGH.
HEH

飢餓苦畜生
逼迫苦黄泉

煩苦餓息
飢餓苦畜生
逼迫苦黄泉

CRACKLE
CRACKLE
CRACKLE
!

!!!
TSUBAKI !
GORŌ!
TASUKE!
EVERYONE !!

WHA

RIGHT. THAT'S EVERY-ONE.
LET'S REPORT TO THE CHIEF.
...BUDDHA...

...THESE CHILDREN HAVE SUFFERED TOO MUCH...
...PLEASE GRANT THEM A HAPPIER FUTURE...
PLEASE GIVE THEM...
...YOUR PROTECTION ...

AAAAA

...WHY ?!
WHY HAVE YOU ABANDONED THESE CHILDREN ...?!
...YOU TOO, PRIEST.

WHEN YOU SCOLD, YOU HAVE TO MAKE YOURSELF AN OGRE AND SCOLD WELL!
YOUR FACE IS TOO KIND, FOR STARTERS...
...
GNG
SOOO

THEN ...
FIVE YEARS LATER ...
PLEASE... I WAS WRONG...
I BEG YOU... DON'T KILL ME!
MSH
NAMU...
FOR-GIVE ...
...ME ...
MSH
...AMIDA BUTSU.

...DO YOU UNDER-STAND ...?
PRAYERS AND WISHES DON'T SAVE ANYTHING.
GRIP
ALL THAT MATTERS IS THE MISSION...
TO SAVE THIS WORLD NOT WORTH SAVING...!!
"MYŌ-Ō THE ANGRY" CANNOT LOSE...
...NOT TILL THOSE CHILDREN RIDE THE WHEEL OF REINCARNATION AND LIVE AGAIN!

READ
THIS
WAY

ANJI!

STAY BACK...
SANO...
TP

ZIP

HE CAN NO LONGER BE REASONED WITH.
HE CAN BE STOPPED ONLY BY FISTS.

SO COME, ANJI!
I'LL ANSWER WITH THOSE FISTS!
GIIIN

The Secret Life of Characters (34)

—Tsubaki and the Children—

First I developed Anji's past, and then the other characters came out of that.

Originally, I was thinking about an entire orphanage (rather than just five orphans), but since that would have been a hassle to draw, this is how it came out. (And still it was a lot of work. Apologies to the assistants!)

I've gotten the comment, "Anji is like the character 'Colossus' in the 'Fatal Attraction' story arc of 'X-Men.'" I can see the similarity, but Anji was created over a year ago, and Watsuki read "X-Men: Fatal Attraction (Japanese Version)" after that, so it wasn't an influence. I do definitely think the flow is similar. Watsuki loves "X-Men," and in this case, "love" may mean more to feel "simpatico" with.

I've also gotten letters saying, "I think Tsubaki 'liked' the priest." Watsuki doesn't disagree. When writing tragic episodes such as this—when laying it all out in my head—I get really emotionally involved and look at it subjectively, and so at first, it flows very easily. But then when it comes to the point, as a writer, that I have to look at it *objectively*, there will always be some hurdles, requiring a tremendous amount of energy to get through. I do feel, having done this episode, that stories are better when they have a lighter tone, and happier content.

There are no models in terms of design. Some people have said Tsubaki looks like "Kusanagi Kyō" from "King of Fighters," but that's a wrong way to look at it. Let's both try and be more literal about this, huh? (Heh.)

Tsubaki's headband is something I put on her mostly to distinguish her from Megumi and Kaoru; there's no other meaning to it. (Oh, but I guess I *did* look into a fashion magazine for it, so maybe you could say the fashion magazine was the model.)

Act 111—Conversation of the Fists
HYOOOH
RIP
RIP
RIP
RIP
RIP

Act 111

Conversation of the Fists

READ THIS WAY

HOOH

GUH!
NNG!

HYOH!!
WHAT'S HAPPENING?
THEY'RE HITTING EACH OTHER WITH THE MASTERY OF TWO LAYERS, BUT NEITHER IS FALLING.

NO. EITHER MAY FALL AT ANY TIME.
BUT THEY'RE BOTH ALSO FIGHTING WITH THEIR *WILL NOT TO LOSE.*

THEIR *SPIRITS* HAVE SURPASSED THEIR *BODIES.*

WHEN THE MASTERY OF TWO LAYERS IS NO LONGER THE DETERMINING FACTOR...
WOK
...THE MATCH IS BASICALLY EQUAL.
THUG WOK
DO YOU REALLY THINK SO?
!
DOESN'T IT BOTHER YOU...
...THAT ALTHOUGH HE'S ONE OF THE JUPPONGATANA, HE'S NOT A SWORDSMAN ?
AND SO WHY THEN DOES HE CARRY A SWORD?
KEEN

BAMMM
!

HH
HH
TSK.
LONG RANGE!!
I SEE...
THAT SWORD IS FOR CONDUCTING THE MASTERY OF TWO LAYERS INTO THE GROUND, TURNING IT INTO AN INDIRECT ATTACK.
THIS IS IT!
THAT BIRDHEAD CAN'T ATTACK FROM OUTSIDE HIS FIGHTING DISTANCE!

HH
HH
HYOH!!
JUMP, SANO!!

READ THIS WAY
HE SAW IT COMING!
HOOH!

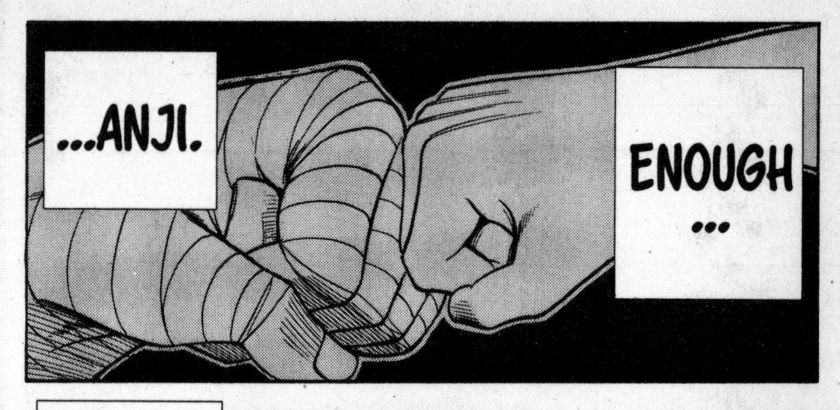
ENOUGH...
...ANJI.

YOU'VE SUFFERED MORE THAN ANYONE SHOULD.
THIS IS AS GOOD A TIME AS ANY TO END YOUR WOUND-FILLED LIFE.

WOUNDS DO NOT MATTER. ALREADY I FEEL NO PAIN.
I WILL CONTINUE TO FIGHT AS THE "BRIGHT KING" UNTIL MY MISSION IS ACCOMPLISHED.

THE CHILDREN WHO SUFFERED AND DIED IN THE FLAMES...
...NEED THIS FROM ME!!

YOU...
...COLOSSAL FOOL!!

YOU DON'T UNDER-STAND ...
...ANYTHING!!

READ THIS WAY
ZUDDBDD
TM

!!!
THAT WAS ...
HE STRUCK WITH HIS FIVE FINGERS ATOP THE MASTERY OF TWO LAYERS!
HE JUST CREATED ...
THE "MASTERY OF THREE LAYERS"!

NNNN...
YAAH!
THOSE DEAD CHILDREN DON'T *WANT* YOUR *MISSION!*
!
THEY ONLY WANT THE *PRIEST* WHO TOOK CARE OF THEM TO BE *HAPPY!*
LOOK!

DRENCHED IN YOUR OWN BLOOD...
...THEY'RE CRYING OUT IN PAIN!

YOU LOVED THEM SO MUCH...
...THAT YOUR SOUL WAS WARPED WHEN YOU LOST THEM.
LISTEN ...
...TO THEIR SPIRITS.

To Be Continued in Vol. 14:
The Time Is Now

The Secret Life of Characters (28)

AMENDMENT

—Yūkyūzan Anji—

Looking back on Anji's story now, I would really have to say that, back then, I was immature as a writer.

Reader response was mostly positive, but the story itself has been significantly cut back from how it was first imagined. I got carried away and kept writing, and then before I knew it, I already had five weeks' worth of story. If I'd kept on with it, it would have interrupted the flow of the fighting to come, so cutting was necessary (in the original version, there was a part where Anji's heart stopped momentarily, because of the "Mastery of Three Layers" thing).

I touched on this a bit in the last "Secret Life." Laying out a story is so, so fun...but then, when it comes to carrying it out, it's so, so hard. If you read into the story deeply enough, you'll agree that, even after all this, Anji's soul has yet to be saved. His rampage toward the dark side has been stopped, and there the story ends....

There's a quote Watsuki thought made so much sense when he first came across it: "Humans are beings who can work all their lives and, with luck, save maybe one other person." (I think it might have been in connection with a religious-themed essay about the "Ohm" incident.) I feel deeply that this applies not only to reality, but to the universe of manga, too. This doesn't mean I'm giving up, though—I may not have anything specific on Anji's later adventures yet, but slowly I *am* seeing the plot, and when the chance presents itself, I'll write it down. Although...you never know...it may turn out to be yet another sad story....

Rurouni Kenshin

GLOSSARY of the RESTORATION

A brief guide to select Japanese terms used in **Rurouni Kenshin**. *Note that, both here and within the story itself, all names are Japanese style—i.e., last or "family" name first, with personal or "given" name following. This is both because* **Kenshin** *is a "period" story, as well as to decrease confusion—if we were to take the example of Kenshin's* sakabatô *and "reverse" the format of the historically established assassin-name "Hitokiri Battôsai," for example, it would make little sense to then call him "Battôsai Himura."*

Fudô Myô-ô
In Vajrayana Buddhism, the destroyer of delusion and protector of Buddhism. Also known in Sanskrit as "the Immovable One," his immovability refers to his ability to remain "unmoved" by carnal temptations. His fearsome blue visage is typically surrounded by flames, representing the purification of the mind.

Hijikata Toshizô
Historically, Vice-Commander of the ***Shinsengumi***

Hiten Mitsurugi-ryû
Kenshin's sword technique, used more for defense than offense. An "ancient style that pits one against many," it requires exceptional speed and agility to master.

hitokiri
An assassin. Famous swordsmen of the period were sometimes thus known to adopt "professional" names—***Kawakami Gensai***, for example, was also known as "Hitokiri Gensai."

Ishin Shishi
Loyalist or pro-Imperialist ***patriots*** who fought to restore the Emperor to his ancient seat of power

Juppongatana
Written with the characters for "ten" and "swords," Shishio's Juppongatana are literally that—the ten generals or "swords" he plans to use in his overthrow of Japan

kanji
Japanese system of writing, based on Chinese characters

aku
Kanji character for "evil," worn by Sanosuke as a remembrance of his beloved, betrayed Captain Sagara and the Sekihô Army

Bakumatsu
Final, chaotic days of the Tokugawa regime

Boshin War
Civil war of 1868-69 between the new government and the ***Tokugawa Bakufu***. The anti-Bakufu, pro-Imperial side (the Imperial Army) won, easily defeating the Tokugawa supporters.

-chan
Honorific. Can be used either as a diminutive (e.g., with a small child—"Little Hanako or Kentarô"), or with those who are grown, to indicate affection ("My dear...").

dojo
Martial-arts training hall

-dono
Honorific. Even more respectful than ***-san***; the effect in modern-day Japanese conversation would be along the lines of "Milord So-and-So." As used by Kenshin, it indicates both respect and humility.

Edo
Capital city of the ***Tokugawa Bakufu***; renamed ***Tokyo*** ("Eastern Capital") after the Meiji Restoration

sakabatô
Reversed-edge sword (the dull edge on the side the sharp should be, and vice versa); carried by Kenshin as a symbol of his resolution never to kill again

-sama
Honorific. The respectful equivalent of ***-san***, ***-sama*** is used primarily in addressing persons of much higher rank than one's self...or, in a romantic sense, in addressing those upon whom one is crushing, wicked hard.

-san
Honorific. Carries the meaning of "Mr.," "Ms.," "Miss," etc., but used more extensively in Japanese than its English equivalent (note that even an enemy may be addressed as "***-san***").

Shinsengumi
Elite, notorious, government-sanctioned and exceptionally skilled swordsman-supporters of the military government (***Bakufu***) which had ruled Japan for nearly 250 years, the Shinsengumi ("newly selected corps") were established in 1863 to suppress the ***loyalists*** and to restore law and order to the blood-soaked streets of ***Kyoto***.

shôgun
Feudal military ruler of Japan

shôgunate
See ***Tokugawa Bakufu***

Tokugawa Bakufu
Military feudal government which dominated Japan from 1603 to 1867

Tokyo
The renaming of "***Edo***" to "***Tokyo***" is a marker of the start of the Meiji Restoration

Kawakami Gensai
Real-life, historical inspiration for the character of *Himura Kenshin*

kenjutsu
The art of fencing; sword-arts; kendô

Komei, Shokatsuryo
Famed Chinese strategist

-kun
Honorific. Used in the modern day among male students, or those who grew up together, but another usage—the one you're more likely to find in Rurouni Kenshin—is the "superior-to-inferior" form, intended as a way to emphasize a difference in status or rank, as well as to indicate familiarity or affection.

Kyoto
Home of the Emperor and imperial court from A.D. 794 until shortly after the ***Meiji Restoration*** in 1868

loyalists
Those who supported the return of the Emperor to power; ***Ishin Shishi***

Meiji Restoration
1853-1868; culminated in the collapse of the ***Tokugawa Bakufu*** and the restoration of imperial rule. So called after Emperor Meiji, whose chosen name was written with the characters for "culture and enlightenment."

Okashira
Literally, "the head"; i.e., leader, boss

Oniwabanshû
Elite group of onmitsu or "spies" of the ***Edo*** period, also known as ninja or shinobi.

patriots
Another term for ***Ishin Shishi***...and, when used by Sano, not a flattering one

rurouni
Wanderer, vagabond

IN THE NEXT VOLUME...

Kenshin—accompanied by Sanosuke and Saitô—squares off against Shinomori Aoshi, former *Okashira* or "head" of the Kyoto-based spy clan, the Oniwabanshû. Bound by promises to both return Misao's "Aoshi-sama" to her safely, as well as to face Shinomori himself in a climactic, decisive battle, the time is now to learn once and for all who has the will to live, who has the will to die...and who has the will to fight.

Available in May 2005

It's Ichigo vs. Menos Grande, the largest Hollow in the Universe!
BLEACH
ブリーチ
Vol. 6 on sale April 5, 2005!
Only $7.95 Each!
Vol. 1-5 on sale now!
on sale now at
www.shonenjump.com
Also available at your local bookstore, comic store and Suncoast Motion Picture Company.
COMIC SHOP LOCATOR SERVICE
888-COMIC-BOOK
888-266-4226
SHONEN JUMP
GRAPHIC NOVELS
VIZ
BLEACH © 2001 by TITE KUBO / SHUEISHA Inc.

Shaman King
EVIL NECROMANCERS!
SHAMAN SNOWBOARDERS!
THE SHAMAN FIGHT
HAS BEGUN
Shaman King
Hiroyuki Takei
volume 5
VOL. 1-5
ON SALE
NOW!
SHONEN JUMP
GRAPHIC NOVELS
SHAMAN KING © 1998 by HIROYUKI TAKEI / SHUEISHA Inc.
Covers subject to change

NARUTO
The Journeyman Ninja Exam continues...in the Forest of Death!
Vol. 6 on sale April 5, 2005!
NARUTO 6 Masashi Kishimoto
Only $7.95 Each!
Vol. 1-5 on sale now!
on sale now at
www.shonenjump.com
Also available at your local bookstore, comic store and Suncoast Motion Picture Company.
COMIC SHOP LOCATOR SERVICE
888-COMIC-BOOK
888-266-4226
SHONEN JUMP
GRAPHIC NOVELS
VIZ

COMPLETE OUR SURVEY AND LET US KNOW WHAT YOU THINK!

☐ Please do NOT send me information about VIZ and SHONEN JUMP products, news and events, special offers, or other information.

☐ Please do NOT send me information from VIZ's trusted business partners.

Name: ______________________________

Address: ______________________________

City: ______________ **State:** ________ **Zip:** ______________

E-mail: ______________________________

☐ **Male** ☐ **Female** **Date of Birth** (mm/dd/yyyy): ___/___/_____ (**Under 13? Parental consent required**)

1 Do you purchase SHONEN JUMP Magazine?

☐ Yes ☐ No **(if no, skip the next two questions)**

If **YES**, do you subscribe?

☐ Yes ☐ No

If **NO**, how often do you purchase SHONEN JUMP Magazine?

☐ 1-3 issues a year

☐ 4-6 issues a year

☐ more than 7 issues a year

2 Which SHONEN JUMP Graphic Novel did you purchase? (please check one)

☐ Beet the Vandel Buster ☐ Bleach ☐ Dragon Ball

☐ Dragon Ball Z ☐ Hikaru no Go ☐ Knights of the Zodiac

☐ Naruto ☐ One Piece ☐ Rurouni Kenshin

☐ Shaman King ☐ The Prince of Tennis ☐ Ultimate Muscle

☐ Whistle! ☐ Yu-Gi-Oh! ☐ YuYu Hakusho

☐ Other ______________________

Will you purchase subsequent volumes?

☐ Yes ☐ No

3 How did you learn about this title? (check all that apply)

☐ Favorite title ☐ Advertisement ☐ Article

☐ Gift ☐ Read excerpt in SHONEN JUMP Magazine

☐ Recommendation ☐ Special offer ☐ Through TV animation

☐ Website ☐ Other ______________________

4 Of the titles that are serialized in SHONEN JUMP Magazine, have you purchased the Graphic Novels?

☐ Yes ☐ No

If **YES**, which ones have you purchased? (check all that apply)

☐ Dragon Ball Z ☐ Hikaru no Go ☐ Naruto ☐ One Piece
☐ Shaman King ☐ Yu-Gi-Oh! ☐ YuYu Hakusho

If **YES**, what were your reasons for purchasing? (please pick up to 3)

☐ A favorite title ☐ A favorite creator/artist ☐ I want to read it in one go
☐ I want to read it over and over again ☐ There are extras that aren't in the magazine
☐ The quality of printing is better than the magazine ☐ Recommendation
☐ Special offer ☐ Other

If **NO**, why did/would you not purchase it?

☐ I'm happy just reading it in the magazine ☐ It's not worth buying the graphic novel
☐ All the manga pages are in black and white unlike the magazine
☐ There are other graphic novels that I prefer ☐ There are too many to collect for each title
☐ It's too small ☐ Other ______________________________

5 Of the titles NOT serialized in the Magazine, which ones have you purchased?
(check all that apply)

☐ Beet the Vandel Buster ☐ Bleach ☐ Dragon Ball
☐ Knights of the Zodiac ☐ The Prince of Tennis ☐ Rurouni Kenshin
☐ Whistle! ☐ Other __________ ☐ None

If you did purchase any of the above, what were your reasons for purchase?

☐ A favorite title ☐ A favorite creator/artist
☐ Read a preview in SHONEN JUMP Magazine and wanted to read the rest of the story
☐ Recommendation ☐ Other

Will you purchase subsequent volumes?

☐ Yes ☐ No

6 What race/ethnicity do you consider yourself? (please check one)

☐ Asian/Pacific Islander ☐ Black/African American ☐ Hispanic/Latino
☐ Native American/Alaskan Native ☐ White/Caucasian ☐ Other

THANK YOU! Please send the completed form to:

VIZ Survey
42 Catharine St.
Poughkeepsie, NY 12601

All information provided will be used for internal purposes only. We promise not to sell or otherwise divulge your information.